HEALING YOURSELF
with Wishful Thinking

ARTHUR BLOCH

HEALING YOURSELF
with Wishful Thinking

Ten Speed Press
Berkeley / Toronto

Ten Speed Press
P.O. Box 7123
Berkeley, California 94707
www.tenspeed.com

Distributed in Australia by Simon and Schuster Australia, in Canada by Ten Speed Press
Canada, in New Zealand by Southern Publishers Group, in South Africa by Real Books, in
Southeast Asia by Berkeley Books, and in the United Kingdom and Europe by Airlift Book
Company.

Cover and Interior Design by Elsewhere Creative

Library of Congress Cataloging-in-Publication Data

Bloch, Arthur, 1948-
  Healing yourself with wishful thinking / by Arthur Bloch.
     p. cm.
  ISBN 1-58008-440-0
  1. Self-care, Health--Humor. 2. Self-help techniques--Humor. I.Title.
  PN6231.S489 B59 2002
  818'.5402--dc21

                         2002007558

First printing, 2002

Printed in the United States of America

1 2 3 4 5 6 7 8 9 10 — 05 04 03 02

To the guests of *Thinking Allowed*, whose depth of understanding and compassion, I hope, will allow them to appreciate this work in the spirit in which it is offered.

What people are saying about
Healing Yourself with Wishful Thinking

"I have tried every form of alternative medicine I could think of to cure my foot fungus. *Wishful Thinking* is the only thing that has worked. Thank you. Thank you. Thank you."
—B. H., Chicago, IL

"Just when I thought nothing would ever go right in my life, along came your *Wishful Thinking* book. Now everything is rosy. I think they will let me out soon."
—R. T., Napa, CA

"Who knew what a powerful cure *Wishful Thinking* could be. If someone had told me, I would have thought it was just wishful thinking."
—J. Q., Wichita, KS

"I lost my little finger when I was just a child. Since using your *Wishful Thinking* program, I'm sure I can see the stub beginning to grow."
—L. S., Manchester, UK

"Your 'never-minding' technique worked for me from the minute I tried it. I can't even remember what I just said."
—K. M., Los Angeles, CA

"After attending your *Wishful Thinking* seminar I tried wing-walking, which I'd always wanted to do. The doctors say that I am very lucky to have survived, but I know it wasn't luck."
—O. T., Milan, Italy

"Last year I stood on my head so much that my chakras got all jumbled together. Thanks to your book I now have them back in the right order."
—S. W., Sedona, AZ

"When my girlfriend left me, I tried every recovery technique I could find. Nothing worked until I tried your step-by-step 'blame-fixing' method. Thank you."
—B. L., Las Vegas, NV

Contents

Preface

DON'T GET ME WRONG.

I'm not one of those people who think science has all the answers. Or *any* answers to the truly important questions, for that matter. The meaning of life, purpose, volition, free will, intention, why women find John Malkovich attractive—these are all issues that might forever be beyond scientific explanation.

Regarding health and wellness, the subject of this book, who is anyone to say what works and what doesn't? I certainly don't want to take my cues from a medical profession for whom "euphoria" is an adverse reaction.

Still, science does seem to have a role here. Even while we read from one of dozens of online wags on the subject that we have "evolved beyond the need for scientific proof," there is not a single guru, healer, chakra reader, past-life therapist, crystal gazer, vibrational consultant, or spiritual counselor who isn't overjoyed when even a small part of this work is "verified" by scientific experiment.

When the Catholic Church turns to science to authenticate the Shroud of Turin, we realize that the mantle of authority has officially passed from the faith-based arbiters of truth to those of the scientific establishment.

And yet we retain the right to our unscientific beliefs.

An Internet search for web pages concerning chakras yields 120,000 choices; for channeling, 118,000; reincarnation, 144,000; karma, 415,000; astrology, 1,060,000; and for angels, a whopping 2,070,000 pages.

So if science is the authority, there is no shortage of antiauthoritarian sentiment.

My own background puts me in a position to appreciate both the joys and the pitfalls of the self-help, New Age, and recovery movements. As producer of the *Thinking Allowed* public television series for sixteen years, I have met and conversed with hundreds of prominent, intelligent writers and thinkers in the areas of psychology, philosophy, personal and spiritual development, and the frontiers of science. On the other hand, as author of ten *Murphy's Law* books, I am a professional curmudgeon whose job it is to poke fun at the hypocrisies and ludicrosities of modern life.

What I've learned is that much serious, intelligent research is being done in alternative areas of study, subjects outside the self-imposed limits of academia and establishment science. There's also a lot of foolery going on in the name of higher truth, a lot of oversimple platitudes masquerading as spirituality, overamped rhetoric in the name of wisdom, and over-the-top claptrap about how you and I should live our lives.

So what is this book about? It's about how far from reality we can stray in service of our search for meaning. It's about the cockamamy things we can convince ourselves of when we hang out with others of like mind. It's about the things people will do and say to make a buck, to make a book, to gain acceptance, to gain control, or to set themselves apart from the rest of the ignorant masses.

But mostly, it's about not taking ourselves so seriously.

—Arthur Bloch
   Oakland, California

1

Relax and Meditate

The Empty Head

THIS VOLUME contains exercises and hints to help you achieve optimum health, happiness, and well-being, all with a minimum of effort and little if any personal responsibility. You'll find the exercises work best when you are comfortable and relaxed. Experts in these matters agree that such procedures are most effective when your defenses are down and your powers of reason and common sense are at rest.

In this chapter we will introduce a simple technique for inducing a receptive, creative, and altogether noncritical mindset that you will find invaluable for the visualization, intuition, and other exercises to follow.

Whether you simply relax or go for the technically more challenging state we call "meditation" is up to you. Relaxation and meditation are essentially indistinguishable from the outside. Other people can't tell, so they have to take your word for it. The two are frequently indistinguishable from the inside as well, so this is an area where a little self-delusion can go a long way.

Surely there are important differences between meditation and merely closing your eyes to rest. Some meditative postures are so excruciating as to preclude any thought of relaxing. And some relaxed positions—such as lying on your back and snoring—won't fool anybody.

But by and large, it doesn't matter for our purposes whether you are truly meditating or just visiting the ashram in hopes of getting laid. You don't have to achieve any metaphysically altered or blissful state to perform the practices described herein. You need only dismiss your critical faculties and hire some easily manipulable stooges to run the show for a while.

CULTIVATING NONBEING

To be truly open to the benefits of wishful thinking, you must give up trying to control everything. You must open yourself to a higher power. Namely, me. This shouldn't be much of a sacrifice. If you were any good at controlling your life, you wouldn't be reading a book like this in the first place.

It is time to relinquish authority over your inner being.

Hand it over.

There. That wasn't so bad, was it?

Now, get down on your knees and bark like a dog.

Just kidding.

Here is the general relaxation procedure we will use throughout this book:

1. First, find a comfortable position, either sitting up, lying down, or leaning against the wall with a cigarette dangling from your lips.

2. Uncross your arms, your legs, your fingers, and your toes. You didn't even realize they were crossed, did you? Now uncross the ones you missed.

3. Close your eyes. You don't really want to watch this.

4. Breathe, if you are not already doing so.

5. Count down from 1,987 using only prime numbers. Alternatively, you can recite *pi* until you pass out (3.14159265358979323846264333392795 . . .).

6. Allow your mind to go away. Do not try to follow.

7. Experience yourself bathed in a brilliant pool of light flowing all around you. If this doesn't work, forget it and move to step 8.

8. Visualize yourself sitting right in front of you, visualizing yourself sitting right in front of you, visualizing yourself sitting right in front of you, etc.

9. Breathe again. It's been a while.

10. Now what do you want to do?

Affirmations

- *I will cultivate mindlessness.*

- *I look cool when I'm meditating.*

- *I can take anything if I'm lying down.*

- *Nothing bad can happen to me while I'm relaxed.*

2

Visualize This

Create as You Go

THE POWER OF visualization to effect positive change in your life, if difficult to document, is well attested to in the literature. Imagery techniques are used by everyone from professional athletes, actors, and artists to therapists, trainers, midwives, and multilevel marketers. Even many doctors and psychiatrists, when pressed, admit that it couldn't hurt.

According to the literature, you can use visualization to contact your higher self, open your energy centers, meet your guardian angel, find hidden treasure, attract a lover, become more popular, reduce stress, relieve pain, increase your self-esteem, feel more youthful, locate missing objects, improve your study habits, clear up your complexion, assuage your grief, strengthen your aura, attract riches, cure depression, lose weight, grow hair, quit smoking, lower your handicap, strengthen your immune system, and heal yourself of everything from hemorrhoids to cancer.

Can we, in fact, create reality through conscious imagination? Does form follow idea? Is the universe really that obliging? These questions are too profound for *Wishful Thinking* to provide a definitive answer.

But surely there's nothing wrong with creating a clear picture of what you'd like to see occur in your life, and there's no shortage of books, videos, and audiotapes that will show you how to do this.

Here is our step-by-step guide:

1. Close your eyes and relax using the progressive relaxation techniques you learned in chapter 1.

2. Create an image in your mind of your favorite bookstore.

3. Visualize a special sale on visualization and creative imagery books and tapes.[1]

4. Go buy some.

You see, so many successful, well-meaning people have invested so much time and energy into this issue that there is little for us to add.

---

1. Be sure that you do not visualize a bargain remainder table. Authors hate that.

Except . . .

NEVER-MINDING

What happens when you try to change the world through visualization and nothing changes? Or what do you do when you try to visualize positive changes and yet things seem to be occurring in the opposite direction?

The worst thing you can do is blame yourself. There's a good chance you're not responsible. And in a situation like this, it's difficult to blame anyone else.

When it becomes evident that your visualization efforts are not having the intended effect, your best bet is to practice a technique we shall call "never-minding."[2]

Never-minding is sort of denial lite. (See chapter 11, Positive Forgetfulness.) Why bother denying something when you can just pooh-pooh it? It is very closely related to glossing-over, and akin, as well, to selective memory, both of which will be discussed elsewhere in this book.

The best sort of positive feedback you can give yourself is to ignore the negative feedback, and an active ability to never-mind is the most valuable tool for doing this.

2. Now that the "verbing" of the English language is almost complete (more than 2,500 web pages include a reference to "languaging"), it is time to begin applying the procedure to two- and three-word phrases. This is our humble contribution.

FOR THE GOOD OF US ALL

Most books and tapes about visualization will tell you that visualization techniques can only be used for good purposes, and that the Laws of Karma will quickly chew up and spit out anyone who attempts to use such techniques for harmful ends.

Do you believe this? If so, *Wishful Thinking* wouldn't presume to tell you otherwise.

What it comes down to is the age-old question of good versus evil against the New Age precept that good conquers all.

We hope you're right.

Affirmations

- *I am all-powerful.*
- *I can do anything I set my mind to.*
- *I will ignore all evidence to the contrary.*

3

Your Wish Is Your Command

Be Careful What You Ask For

WAIT A SECOND! Let us assume, for the sake of discussion, that it is indeed possible to affect the world just by consciously visualizing the changes you want. Then what about the rest of the crap you think about over the course of the day?

If the power of your imagination is strong enough to create what you want in life, isn't it also powerful enough to create what you *don't* want? Aren't your fears, nightmares, and other horrible imaginings just as capable of manifesting themselves in the world as your positive thoughts?

Well, yes. Unless you're able to impose some kind of "hierarchy of values" on your mental meanderings.

The first step is to become aware of your negative mental activity. For some, this can be a full-time job. Be sure you don't get down on yourself for having negative thoughts because that, too, is a negative thought. This is called a negative feedback loop. It's like a whirlpool. Don't go near it.

Okay. Now you're in the whirlpool. At this point, the best thing to do is to let go and enjoy the ride. When you come out the other side, we'll try something else.

Whee!

META-REPROGRAMMING

The most effective way to proceed is to follow a step-by-step procedure for reprogramming yourself, with a goal of overriding the negative consequences of your mental imagery.

To begin, assume the position (i.e., follow the relaxation procedure in chapter 1, Relax and Meditate). Then follow these simple steps in order:

1. Establish complete and total control over your emotions, your thoughts, your desires, your weaknesses, your stray thoughts, images, and so on.

2. Generate a meta-thought as follows: "Only my positive, life-affirming thoughts, feelings, and images will manifest in the world. This thought form will have priority over all thoughts, feelings, and images from step 1."

3. Enter a password to protect this meta-thought. Write it down somewhere and put it where you won't find it when you're in a bad mood and might be tempted to tamper with your meta-thought.

By utilizing this simple procedure you can ensure that only your positive thoughts will become manifest in the world, and you can trust yourself to venture forth without leaving a trail of disaster in your wake.

Affirmations

- *Only good can come of this.*

- *I am a source of positive vibes.*

- *I am in complete control.*

- *I am not responsible for anything bad that happens.*

4

Preparing Your Sanctuary

Creating a Special Place

ALMOST ALL OF THE self-help and visualization guidebooks recommend that you create a "special place," or imaginary inner sanctuary, to visit during your meditations. This is a sort of virtual vacation home designed to your specifications, where you can go at a moment's notice and they can't kick you out.

It is a place of peace and tranquility, warmth and comfort. Except for your various guides, angels, and totems, there won't be anyone else around in your special place to know what you're up to there.

Sometimes a special place is outdoors, like a meadow or a beachfront property—though the latter can be quite expensive. Waterfalls and babbling brooks are popular, as are caves, grottoes, mountaintops, gardens, and redwood groves.

More often your special place is a room or chamber in a house, a castle, a library, a church, or a temple. It can really be anywhere, someplace you've been or someplace you'd like to be. I know a fellow whose special place is a room in Drew Barrymore's house. It's up to you.

If you can't afford a special place, you might consider a time-share. Or perhaps you could create a virtual mobile home.

OUTFITTING YOUR SPACE

The more realistic and detailed your sanctuary, the more comfortable you will be during your sessions and the longer you'll be apt to stay. It is therefore a good idea to provide for certain creature comforts in anticipation of your virtual needs.

Why not install that media center you can't afford in real life? The large screen will come in handy for your visualization exercises.

A fully equipped bar would be nice. Help you relax. And a drug stash isn't illegal here. You might want to create a hidey hole to use if you want to conceal something from your higher self or your inner child.

This might be the only place you'll ever be where a waterbed is appropriate.

Whether you want bathroom facilities is up to you. It's not always a good idea to relieve yourself while your actual body is sitting around somewhere fully clothed.

It's also handy to equip your special place with various creative tools, paints and brushes, pencils, musical instruments—all of those things that intimidate you in actual life.

ALTERNATIVE VISIONS

For some of you, these real-world trappings are the last thing you'd want in your sanctuary. You might want to fill it instead with incense and candles, exotic rugs, kilim pillows, and fringed cushions.

I hope you're not one of those people whose special place is a spartan room with a grass mat on a hard floor, nothing on the walls, and no distractions. This is supposed to be someplace you *want* to go. Why not design yourself a torture chamber while you're at it?

Some visioneers like to have more then one special place to visit according to their mood or purpose. These places might be separate, existing in different imaginary worlds, or connected by a doorway, path, hallway, tunnel, or by chutes and ladders.

Your place can grow and change over time. These days, of course, you'll want high-speed Internet access.

As you refine your powers of imagination, you'll find that there are no limits to what you can have or do in your special place. It's just that you don't want your actual life to seem so pale in comparison that you won't want to come back.

Affirmations

- *I can do anything in my special place.*

- *Whatever happens here is right and good.*

- *My special place is nicer than yours.*

5

Setting Goals

. . . and Moving Them Back

SO FAR WE'VE BEEN wandering peacefully through the varieties of wishful behavior. We have talked of visualizing what we want and imagining the world as we'd like it to be. And we've been learning ways to keep believing in our personal dreams in the face of the evidence.

When you're ready to get real, at some point it will become necessary to set certain clear goals for yourself. Unless you define your aims and purposes, you will never know for sure whether your visualization efforts have been having any effect at all. (If you'd rather not know, you can skip this chapter altogether.)

Setting goals is a tricky business. For one thing, when you ask yourself why you want something, you can't just stop there. Whatever your purpose, there is always a higher purpose.

Why do I want a new job? So I will earn more money. Why do I want more money? So I can be more independent. Why be independent? So I can spend more time doing what I want. And what do I want to do? . . .

True goals are always receding.

Whether your highest purpose is to know yourself, to know God, or to be God, whether it's to get well, to get rich, or to get laid, it's frequently not the first thing you think of when you ask yourself what you want.

MAKING A CHOICE

People who are deeply into goal setting often break down their goal lists into seemingly manageable areas, such as work and career, relationships, money, creativity, travel, and leisure. They usually throw in something about world peace or the environment, so it doesn't all seem so selfish.

In fact, when you ask yourself what you want in any of these categories you quickly begin to include things that have as much chance of happening as, well, world peace.

So before you make a list of your goals, you should ask yourself this: *Do I really want to write down in no uncertain terms my deepest aims and aspirations? Am I willing to face the possibility that, having set down what I'm really after, I am unlikely to achieve even a small part of it?*

GOAL-TENDING

If you decide to go ahead and list your goals, there are various steps you can take to protect yourself from failure.

- Make sure not to tell anyone about your goals.

- Make up simple, inane goals that (a) are easy to attain or (b) you don't care whether you reach or not.

- Write them down illegibly, perhaps with your wrong hand.

- Write down your goals after the fact, including only those you've accomplished.

- Set as one of your goals "rising above goal-oriented behavior."

- Apply to your unmet goals one of the never-minding techniques described elsewhere in this volume.

- Manage to lose your list.

All of these measures will allow you to feel that you are practicing the most sophisticated of self-help techniques. At the same time you will be protecting yourself from disappointment and unwanted reality checks.

Affirmations

- *I will figure out exactly what I want by next week.*

- *I only want what I already have.*

- *I'm not really into goals, anyway.*

6

Your Spirit Guide

A Voice from Beyond Reason

ALL YOUR LIFE you've been told that people who hear voices are crazy, that people who talk to themselves are disturbed, and that anyone over six years old with an imaginary friend is, well, a little simple.

These days, you are asked not only to engage intentionally in all of the above, but to take as gospel anything that comes out of your spirit guide's imaginary mouth.

In case this notion of inner guides is new to you, here is the premise, as usually stated:

- We all have within us a higher wisdom, an intuitive means of knowing what is right and true.

- We are usually blocked off from this knowledge by (a) our logical mind, (b) the sensory world, or (c) our lack of faith in our own insights.

- We can bypass these blockages by contacting our own higher self in the form of an inner guide, a being of great love, compassion, and knowledge.

- We can meet this guide and hear what he/she has to say by simply relaxing and allowing him/her to appear.

As Mark Twain wrote, "Faith is believin' what you know ain't so." While it is completely in keeping with the tone of this book to accept the above at face value, even the most open-minded among you must realize the pitfalls of believing and acting upon whatever your inner spirit guide might have to say.

This may seem obvious, but *just because you're imagining it doesn't make it real.*

FIRST CONTACT

Let us agree at the start that your inner guide, whom you will be meeting shortly, is a part of your own psyche, albeit a part whose powers of omniscience and prescience have yet to be proven. That is to say it's not some disembodied soul, cosmic being, angel, goddess, demon, or other discarnate or supernatural entity, right?

Okay, then, here's the process:

1. Close your eyes and follow the progressive relaxation directions you learned in chapter 1, Relax and Meditate.

2. If you don't feel too silly doing so, go to your "special place" from chapter 4, Preparing Your Sanctuary.

3. If your sanctuary is indoors, open a door in case your guide is outside somewhere.

4. This is tricky. Your eyes are closed, right? But you're looking around, aren't you? Close your *other* eyes, the ones you're using to look around your special place.

5. Say to yourself, "When I open my eyes my inner guide will be right in front of me, ready to answer any questions I might have and to direct my actions and thoughts toward achieving my goals."

6. Open your "inner" eyes and meet your guide.

Note: When you first meet your inner guide, be sure to check credentials carefully. Ask for references. Many who claim to be your higher self are actually splinter elements of your various sub-personalities seeking a more influential role in your day-to-day decision making.

KNOW YOUR GUIDE

Your guide might appear in any form, male or female, young or old, someone real whom you know and respect, someone who is dead, a fictional character (if this isn't obvious), an animal (at this point a talking animal is hardly putting any additional strain on credulity), a mythological creature, a being of light, or even a mechanical entity.

Beware of guides with eye patches and wooden legs, pointed hats, horns, missing teeth, or festering wounds. While this may seem prejudicial stereotyping, it is your unconscious we're dealing with, and perhaps you're trying to tell yourself something.

Your guide is there to help you, to advise you, to put you in touch with your own true feelings and deep desires.

It's also nice to have someone new to blame when things fail to go as planned.

Affirmations

- *My higher self doesn't know what's going on either.*
- *I will believe everything I can imagine.*
- *Whatever goes wrong, it's my spirit guide's fault.*

7

Vibration, Chakras, and You

Muzak of the Spheres

EVERYTHING VIBRATES. It's one of the things that's wrong with everything. And what's worse, when one thing starts vibrating, it sets other things vibrating.

Most of the time these vibrations are so subtle that they're not worth concerning yourself with, but sometimes they can be a real bother, causing everything from headaches and nosebleeds to avalanches and earthquakes.

Everything that vibrates does so at a particular frequency, from the period of the electron (1.52×10^{-16} seconds) to the Hindu Mahaa Yuga (4,320,000 years). Brainwaves, musical notes, visible light, radio waves, and countless other vibratory phenomena all have their own characteristic frequencies and—since the body is said to be sensitive to things that vibrate—all have been accused of affecting our health and well-being.

The world of the healing arts draws heavily on the various qualities of sound, color, scent, and touch. Healers have happily adopted and applied such scientific principles as sympathetic vibration, resonance, and harmonics to help understand—critics would say to lend credibility to—certain occult and traditional knowledge such as the chakra system, astrology, crystal healing, aromatherapy, and so on. (See chapter 17, Alternative Alternative Medicine.)

Subscribing to this vision of therapeutic vibrational interactions can lead you, at best, into a world of delightful smells, good music, beautiful visuals, and, hopefully, frequent relaxing and pleasant massages. At worst, you can come to believe that everything you hear, smell, touch, and see is having an unknown and probably harmful effect on some obscure internal organ, the existence of which you'd rather not even know about.

CHAKRAS ARE US

At the basis of nearly all vibrational therapy theory is the *chakra system*. Originally a complicated and elaborate component of Hindu cosmology, contemporary healing practice has simplified the system to seven "energy centers" in (or near) the body, each of which can be tweaked and tuned by application of the appropriate color, gemstone, musical note, unguent, herb, essential oil, balm, mineral, flower extract, elixir, fragrance, vowel sound, or mantra.

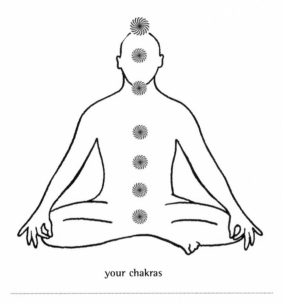

your chakras

To better understand the chakra system, *Wishful Thinking* spent a couple of days on the Internet, exploring a few hundred of the more than 120,000 web pages containing reference to chakras.

You'd be amazed at the variety and ingenuity of products and services being marketed directly to your various chakras—musical tapes for each energy center, chemical patches to apply locally to the chakra areas, chakra-inspired jewelry and clothing, chakra bowls and urns, chakra wallpaper, chakra stones, chakra soaps, chakra balancing kits, chakra repair manuals, chakra bells and gongs, chakra-specific aromatics, crystal resonators, the aforementioned oils and balms, etc. You can even have chakra-related mantras delivered daily to your pager.

Wishful Thinking also learned quite a bit about chakra theory, the gist of which can be found at the end of this chapter. (The quotes are verbatim.)

What we've been unable to find—and not, I swear, for want of looking—is any serious scientific or medical verification of the existence of the chakra system, or even much in the way of studies exploring the issue.

So while the wonders of the mind-body interaction continue to beg for a systematic explanation, it has apparently yet to be confirmed by any objective method that the chakras are the answer we are seeking. And if the original Hindu chakra system hasn't been established as fact, even less so the grossly oversimplified version that is foisted upon us in popular literature or the elaborate chakra-related treatment modalities that one finds in the New Age bazaar.

Still, it is remarkable how deeply the idea of the chakra system has penetrated the popular psyche and been accepted as somehow real, if unverifiable. It may be only a metaphor, as some contend, but it is certainly one of the most well-marketed metaphors to come down the pike.

NEW CHAKRAS FOR THE MILLENNIUM

In accordance with ancient Mayan prophecy, the dawning of the millennium means the awakening of (God forbid) a new New Age. To welcome this era, the human body, in conjunction with the master planners and sponsored by a coalition of major drug companies, is inaugurating several new chakras that existed previously only in the most advanced adepts.

The "Intuition Chakra"

Located in the pit of your stomach, this chakra regulates your sense of what is right and wrong, making you violently ill if you are even thinking about doing something you shouldn't do. It is otherwise known as the "Santa Claus Chakra."

The "Bullshit Chakra"

This chakra, located in your neck, causes you to clear your throat audibly when something seems fishy.

The "Chutzpah Chakra"

Located in your gallbladder, this chakra is aroused when you are vexed by audacious assertions and unmitigated claims.

The "Spam Chakra"

This chakra evolved very quickly since around 1995, when email first began to be used as an advertising medium. Located in your mouse hand, this chakra protects you from unwanted solicitations for penile enlargements, nubile teenage babes, and hot stock tips.

The "Guilt Chakra"

When this chakra is activated, it causes the lowering of the eyes, the reddening of the cheeks, and the shuffling of the feet. There is a "Blame Subchakra" that when fully developed can override the Guilt Chakra and cause turning of the head and pointing of the finger. The Guilt Chakra is located in your mother.

Affirmations

* *Give me a place to put my vibrator and I can move the world.*

* *When I'm really calm, I can feel my chakras.*

* *I have risen above the need for things to make sense.*

Internet Research Results

ON THE NUMBER OF CHAKRAS

"Usually there are said to be seven chakras, but in traditional Hindu philosophy there are really only six."

"There are seven chakras, one for each of the seven bodies we possess."

"Humans have seven major in-body chakras, one minor chakra, and one very important out-of-body chakra."

"Pranic Healing . . . treats eleven major chakras or energy centres of the body."

"My mission is activating the 18 chakras."

"Light Activation of the Twenty Chakra System is part of the stepping up of our vibratory field of energy within ourselves, and with our Mother Earth and all Beings."

"Actually we have 72 Chakras on the body and 22 which we can work with our inner self, including the 7 primary Chakras."

"There are 3 master, 4 major, and over 300 minor chakras in the human body. There are also several non-physical chakras situated outside of the body."

"Old Hindu scripts mention around 88,000 Chakras and 350,000 Nadis in total in one human body!! There are 7 major Chakras and around 40 secondary Chakras . . . All the others are real small."

"As you evolve, you will come to understand that you are one big chakra."

ON THE LOCATION OF CHAKRAS

"The major chakras are related to the endocrine glands. Each endocrine gland is physically closely situated near its associated chakra."

"Not all chakras are situated on the physical body; many are found in the etheric layers of the aura."

"The most important chakras are found in the hands and feet."

"Incarnations in life forms that do not have arms and legs would, understandably, have different chakras."

"We believe that more out-of-body chakras will be discovered in the not-too-distant future."

"The ninth chakra is about four feet above your head."

"The chakras are associated with basic levels of consciousness and are located where the body and mind meet."

ON THE NATURE OF CHAKRAS

"Think of a Chakra as a lightbulb; the resulting light is called an Aura."

"Each chakra [is] a spinning antenna."

"Their function is often described as being like a camera lens."

"Chakras are likened to flowers on a stalk."

"Once activated, the chakras are like beads on a vertical string."

"Think of it as an invisible, rechargeable battery. It is charged and recharged through contact with the stream of cosmic energy in the air."

"Chakras are energy centers which operate like step-down transformers for the higher frequency energies."

"These chakras . . . function as pumps or valves, regulating the flow of energy through our energy system."

"Major chakras are just like power stations that supply vital energy to major and vital organs."

"Your chakras are like funnels, receiving energy from your emotional body and channeling it into your physical body."

"The individual chakras are like gorgeous small bowls."

"Chakras are like flywheels of a gigantic machine."

"The chakras are like the pistons and drive shaft, which enable us to utilize this fire/spirit fuel energy to turn the wheels, i.e. animate matter, the physical body."

"Chakras are like microwave dishes tuning into the energy grid."

"The seven chakras are like the knobs of a radio, which can communicate the multilevels of soul."

"The energy field of the human body has junction boxes in it, like the wiring in a house or the inter-state system of roads which connect the United States. These junction boxes are called chakras."

"I generally refer to them as 'energy substations' much like an electric power plant."

"The chakras are the software, the endocrine glands and brain cells are the hardware, and kundalini delivers the information to the monitor (ego)."

"Our chakras are like floppy disks; they carry all of our programs."

"Chakras are like 'databases' of the human body, storing, transmitting, and receiving vibrational information or light."

8

Accepting Loss and Change

The Comforts of Blame-Fixing

SOMETIMES YOU lose your job. Sometimes your boyfriend leaves you. Sometimes the toilet backs up. Sometimes your car smashes into a fire hydrant. Sometimes your kids use crack.

Face it. These things happen—if not every day, then every other day. You can't fight it. You can't ignore it (unless you're really good at this). And you can't change the way things are (unless you're really, really good at this).

But what you can do is *change your attitude*. That's the one thing that's totally within your purview.

It's your choice. Are you going to allow yourself to be victimized by circumstances? Or are you going to overcome your self-negating tendencies and turn your everyday setbacks into everyday miracles?

Here are the steps involved for dealing with personal loss and misfortune. Before you begin, make yourself extremely comfortable.

1. Use the relaxation techniques developed in chapter 1, Relax and Meditate.

2. If you wish, use the sacred space you created in chapter 4, Preparing Your Sanctuary.

3. Review the sequence of negative events and occurrences. Do not get too attached.

4. Recognize the problem. Keep it from overwhelming you.

5. Explore your feelings about what has happened.

6. Reorganize the facts so that no blame or responsibility lies with you.

7. Allow yourself to blame someone else.

GOOD GRIEF

Grieving isn't fun, no matter what they say. Sometimes, when you're really down, the usual techniques we recommend for feeling better—blaming others or thinking about someone who has it worse than you—simply don't work.

It's generally easy to see the bright side of other people's problems. But it's hard enough in the best of times to see the bright side of your own problems.

Following is a series of steps designed to help you come to terms with the loss of a loved one, a dear pet, an important client, a job, a cherished object, or just about anything else.

Begin by relaxing as described in chapter 1. Then:

1. If it's a cherished object you've lost, try to remember where you last had it. Go there and look for it. Otherwise, proceed to step 2.

2. If you've lost someone dear to you, allow yourself to picture them clearly. Don't try to turn away. It won't work anyway since they're inside your head.

3. Feel their presence. Experience their warmth. Smell their breath. Have they been drinking?

4. Allow yourself to feel your own deep sadness at their passing.

5. Okay, that's enough.

6. Now, did this person (pet) ever do anything really nasty to you?

7. Is there any way in hell that it's your fault they took off?

8. Is there anything that's being blamed on you that you can now blame on them?

9. Did they leave you anything in their will (or on their desk, if they've just fired you)? Skip this step if it's your pet that's gone.

10. What can you do now that you couldn't do while they were around?

11. Is there anyone you can sue?

Knowing what you now know, gently release their image. Retain this awareness as you return to the world.

Affirmations

- *It only appears that things are getting worse.*

- *Accept yourself—blame someone else.*

- *I have transcended gain and loss. I'm broke.*

- *It wasn't my fault.*

9

The Key to Recovery

Get Over It

IF YOU'RE READING this, you're a survivor. Perhaps not of domestic violence or ritual abuse, but you've probably made it through high school and that's bad enough.

These days, when unable to cope with stress, you are likely to be said to have been traumatized, and thus become a candidate for diagnosis and treatment by the recovery experts, be they well-meaning therapists, hard-nosed tough-it-out survivalists, or New Age bliss mongers.

For some reason—and *Wishful Thinking* isn't necessarily knocking it—people in the stress/trauma/survival/recovery business are highly prone to list making: lists of stress factors, lists of symptoms, lists of possible traumas, lists of treatment options, and so on.

For instance, you've almost certainly encountered one of those life-assessment tests that measure the various factors that can lead to stress. Have you recently experienced the loss of a loved one? 12 points. Have you had a major change in your financial situation? 8 points. Are you or someone close to you involved in any legal conflict? 6 points.

These questions are good, and they can scare the daylights out of you, but the truly important issues are never mentioned. Here are a few of the questions they usually omit:

- Have you recently had a really bad haircut? 15 points.

- Did your so-called friends ever "ditch" you when you were a kid? 12 points.

- Did they ever ditch you as an adult? 20 points.

- Did your cat throw up in the middle of the night and you couldn't get back to sleep? 6 points.

- Did your computer crash, causing you to lose valuable data? 8 points.

- Are you gaining weight? 15 points.

- Is your best friend losing weight? 20 points.

Depending on your score, you are deemed more or less likely to exhibit stress-related symptoms and suffer from stress-related ailments.

STRESS POINTS

You can also find lists of these symptoms and ailments. Fatigue, irritability, insomnia, anger, anxiety or panic attacks, and loss of appetite are generally mentioned.

Again, they usually omit some of the most obvious signs that you're stressed out:

- You sleep under the bed.

- You only go to movies when you can have an entire row to yourself.

- You shake uncontrollably at the thought of relaxing.

- You leave messages for yourself in the form of ransom notes.

- You can't remember what you just read.

TRAUMA SIGNALS

Trauma victims often exhibit low self-esteem and self-blame. This manifests in low expectations and other self-deprecating attitudes.

"Victim thinking" includes thoughts such as:

- Nobody loves me. Everybody hates me. I think I'll eat some worms.

- I can't do shit.

- I feel better when I blame myself.

- Even when it seems like I've done something right, it turns out wrong.

- When I do something really right, I have to undo it.

- The only time I'm sure of myself is when I'm sure I'm wrong.

- When I say "Let's forget the whole thing," I can't.

Yet another sign of trauma is survivor guilt. Rather than "there but for the grace of God," it's "Hey, why not me?" To recognize survivor guilt, ask yourself if you ever feel guilty that you're not feeling guilty enough? Or, feel guilty because you know you shouldn't be feeling so guilty? How about feeling good about yourself because you feel guilty?

MOVING ON

As for methodologies for recovery, they are as varied and as list-prone as the testing and diagnosis process.

The traditional therapeutic model for treatment of post-traumatic stress—if you can refer to a tradition in a condition that has only been officially recognized since 1980—involves careful, step-by-step work with professionals trained to be sensitive to the client's needs and ability to make progress toward balance and wholeness.

These steps, which are often painstakingly slow to achieve, include:

- Remembering and reconstructing the trauma
- Feeling your feelings
- Appreciating your progress
- Harnessing your rage
- Avoiding revictimization
- Learning emotional self-care
- Attaining empowerment

The New Age approach to healing is more direct. The following steps to recovery are extracted verbatim from various guides and manuals. You can:

"Beam soothing healing light."

"Work with the perpetrator."

"Tap the experience using the tapping technique."

"Say to yourself, 'I can get through this without anger.'"

"Stand back and view it with the wisdom of your soul."

"Put light around the experience."

"Break a balloon to release the energy."

"Source your self-image."

"Picture the problem dissolving and flowing energy away."

"Send the incident to your recycle bin."[3]

So you see, you don't need to go through that painful therapeutic process at all.

There's one more list of procedures for getting over unpleasant feelings and experiences. Without minimizing the reality of stress-related trauma and the difficulties involved, *Wishful Thinking* suggests you try these first and see if they help:

- Read a mystery.

- Have some ice cream.

- Get some exercise.

- Help somebody.

---

3. I thought I'd invented this myself. See chapter 11, Positive Forgetfulness.

- Go to the beach.

- Rent a comedy.

- Buy yourself a new sweater.

- Go out to dinner.

Affirmations

- *I'm not in touch with my anger. I'm just angry.*

- *I've been over it for a long time, but I enjoy the attention.*

- *I can't remember what it was I was upset about.*

10

Preventing Inner Child Abuse

Enact Your Own Megan's Law

THERE IS TREMENDOUS interest within the "recovery" movement in getting in touch with your inner child, that which is variously described as (a) the playful, joyous, creative, and thus usually repressed side of your personality or (b) the wounded, emotionally underdeveloped, and often destructive sub-personality that persists in almost all of us as a result of a dysfunctional upbringing, a.k.a. childhood.

The inner child is the part of you that:

- Desires to be nurtured, cared for, and loved
- Is a fun-loving, unsophisticated free spirit or pixie that you have tamed and suppressed
- Is emotional, sensitive, and easily hurt or offended

- Is pained, neglected, frustrated, abused, ignored, and hidden from view

- Either grew up too fast or never grew up at all, depending on which model you're using

- Avoids responsibility by claiming that its behavior is a result of stuff that happened so long ago that it's beyond the statute of limitations

- Throws a tantrum whenever it doesn't get its way

You don't need any set of instructions or guided meditations to gain an awareness of your inner child. You only have to look at your behavior the last time you visited your parents.

If you want help, there is no shortage of therapists whose business model is heavily tilted toward inner-child counseling and regression. You can receive such therapy over the phone, by email, or over the Internet.

YOUR INNER GROWN-UP

There is much less interest within the recovery movement in contacting your inner grown-up [4]—the mature, practical, and reasonably sensible side of yourself. This is the part of you that:

---

4. The Internet score: "inner child"—62,800 pages; "inner grown-up"—9 pages.

- Accepts responsibility for its actions

- Can make and keep agreements with others

- Can make long-term plans and is able to put off immediate gratification

- Responds appropriately and in proportion to stimuli

- Is capable of doing things for others without resentment or need for personal gain

- Is neither over-indulgent nor over-disciplined

- Can put aside its own needs for a greater need or greater good

In fairness, inner-child therapists would say that coming to terms with the injured, unfulfilled parts of your psyche is a prerequisite for developing into a balanced, mature, and whole adult. But unless such therapy is conducted thoroughly and professionally, there is a fine line—often no line at all—between acting on behalf of one's inner child and just being childish.

MISS SUB-PERSONALITY

Once you acknowledge the existence of your inner child—and your inner grown-up if you've got one—you are opening (as former New Mexico Governor Bruce King once warned) "a box of pandoras." I am speaking of the wonderful world of sub-personalities.

While some therapists would disagree, many of them find the idea that we are each composed of various "personalities" or personae to be an extremely useful model. Whether this is in fact the true nature of the psyche or rather just a convenient way of approaching the problems of therapeutic intervention is not necessarily of importance.

Note that we are not speaking here of so-called "multiple personality disorder," à la Sybil or (for those like me who've been around too long) Bridey Murphy. Nor are we speaking of schizophrenia, which used to be mistakenly called "split personality."

We are speaking, rather, of the various and often conflicting motivations and urges that make up our workaday existence. In therapy, one is often asked to isolate and act out these urges in an attempt, through understanding and compassion, to comprehend, accept, and ultimately diffuse their unconscious influence.

BACK TO CHILDHOOD

In this context, the inner child is definitely the enfant terrible among the subs, and the one that has received the most press.

There's also a lot of marketing directly to the inner child, and I don't mean Porsches and RAV4s. You can buy lullabies for your inner child, inner-child

T-shirts, inner-child greeting cards and notepads, inner-child meditations and mantras, inner-child coffee mugs (though you would think this would stunt your inner child's growth).

Whether your inner child needs healing and years of therapy or just freedom of expression depends on whom you talk to. As a method for getting us all to lighten up, to play more, to go easier on ourselves, to be more open, and to take ourselves less seriously, the inner child business seems to be of considerable value to a lot of people.

It would be good for all of us to remember, however, that the inner child is often reflected in the world as the outer brat, with whom most of us are in touch all too often.

Affirmations

- *Don't blame me, I'm only a kid.*

- *It's good to be selfish.*

- *It's okay to cry, as long as it makes someone feel guilty.*

- *I will protect my inner child from the part of me that knows better.*

- *I should be waited on hand and foot.*

11

Positive Forgetfulness

Thanks for the Memories . . . Not

LOTS OF HORRIBLE THINGS HAPPEN TO US EVERY DAY.

Or do they?

At the end of the day, are we ever sure what has really occurred? Could I possibly have done that? Did she really say that? Did I really say that?

Now that you think about it, you don't really know, do you? You can't reconstruct your day in anything approaching a complete and accurate rendering, can you? And if you can't remember exactly, maybe you can't remember *at all*. Maybe you're only remembering your reaction to what happened, or your memory of your reaction, or your memory of your memory.

You see what a slippery slope this is. Which gives you lots of wiggle room, doesn't it?

People will tell you that the past is fixed, determined. But there's nothing as malleable, as adjustable to your needs, as a foggy memory.

Use it.

Why is it that your memory gets worse the older you get? It must be because you're *supposed* to forget stuff. With a little practice, you can change your miserable memories into wonderful—if fallacious—ones and be none the wiser. Or, since this comes with age, perhaps that's what wisdom is all about.

If God didn't want us to fudge the facts, why did He give us a failing memory?

SELECTIVE MEMORY

Imagine all your memories lined up like computer files, arranged according to date or file type. (We do not recommend alphabetical sorting for this exercise.)

Now hold down the "control" key (how ironic) and select only those memories that reinforce a positive, affirmative image of yourself and your life.

Now delete all the others. Go ahead. They'll still be in your subconscious (recycle bin) should you ever need them.[5]

We do this all the time. It's called selective memory, and it's how most of us get through the day.

With a little practice, you can learn to:

- Select by theme

- Edit your memories during the selection process

- Selectively retrieve memories from your subconscious to create a desired impression

- Convince yourself of any number of foolish ideas about your personal history

- Perform many other advanced selection options.

CREATIVE MEMORY

Selective memory can take you only so far. What if there's nothing worth selecting? This is why for serious self-helpers *Wishful Thinking* recommends the practice of Creative Memory, the *proactive* approach to memory management.

---

5. Some behaviorists will argue that there's no such thing as the subconscious. What are they on? You can't remember someone's name in the morning. You can remember it in the afternoon. Where was it in the meantime? Duh.

Conscious memory creation isn't always easy, and it's not for everybody. Here's how it works:

Try starting with something small, something you can deceive yourself about without feeling guilt and self-recrimination.

Say, for instance, you're a football fan. Your team lost yesterday. Rather than tell yourself that they won—a memory that will be refuted whenever you see the won-lost record—tell yourself they lost by only three points instead of six. That way, if you ever see the actual score, you can shrug off the discrepancy as unimportant.

It is this ability to ignore discrepancies, which we shall call "glossing-over," that you must learn and cultivate.

In the same way that anything is edible if you chop it finely enough, any memory can become convincing if you break it into small enough "units of plausibility."

Now try this: Imagine the world as you'd like it to be. Okay, got it? Now imagine this as already having happened. Then forget the fact that you imagined it. Things are already the way they should be, and anybody who says otherwise is a liar.

SWIMMING IN DENIAL

As a wit greater than mine has said, denial is not a river in Egypt. What this wiseass failed to tell you is that denial is a powerful tool, an important weapon in the arsenal of positive forgetfulness.

How often have you managed to forget something unpleasant (or not think of it at all) when, out of the blue, something or someone reminds you of the thing you were forgetting?

Here is where a well-developed sense of denial can serve you. Not only can you refuse to acknowledge—even to yourself—that you've thought about this thing, whatever it is, but with a little practice you can deny the thing itself, deny that you find it unpleasant, and even deny that you're in denial.

There is truly no limit to the power of this tool in the art and practice of wishful thinking.

Affirmations

- *I won't trust my memory if I don't like what it's telling me.*

- *I will make up stories, then believe they're true.*

- *If I don't know what just happened, I will see it in the most favorable possible light.*

- *It's not a lie if I'm telling it to myself.*

12

Life Is But a Dream

Is Your Life Based on a True Story?

DREAMS ARE FLEETING. BUT THEN, SO IS THE REST OF LIFE.

You've probably had thousands of dreams over many thousands of nights. How many of them can you remember?

On the other hand (or perhaps on the same hand), what can you recall of the millions of events in your waking life? Of the thousands of days you've spent at work, how many can you remember in any detail? How many books that you've read? How many concerts that you've attended?[6]

---

6. Okay, so maybe there's a reason you can't remember the concerts.

The difference between waking and nonwaking life is vastly overstated. We remember only a small fraction of what we experience. The rest is lost in a dreamlike fog.

If you think you're so smart, if you think you pay attention and retain most of what goes on around you, take this simple quiz:

1. Who is the author of the book you're holding in your hand?

2. What well-known song is the source of the title of this chapter? (Hint: It's not "Sh-boom." That was "Life *could be* a dream.")[7]

3. What did you have for dinner last Tuesday?

4. What was the first question in this list?

As we pointed out in the previous chapter, your life, such as it is, is a series of half-remembered events, reconstructions, wishful misrememberings, and outright fabrications. These are tied together as a story you're telling yourself with you as the central character.

Not everyone's story is a positive one. Our stories are as often tragic or comic as they are heroic. For every person out there who remembers things only in the best possible light, there's some shlump who can remember only the negative.

7. *Row, Row, Row Your Boat*

WAKING UP

Dreams and waking life have one important thing in common. We don't remember anything unless we wake up.

Studies reveal that dreams that occur in the middle of the night, and during which sleep is uninterrupted, are not recalled.

Similarly, we only remember life events during moments of self-awareness—i.e., waking up—though this awareness is usually marginal and momentary at best.

How many times have you been driving your car when you suddenly realize that you've been completely unaware of your surroundings, your own driving, the traffic, or the route you've taken? Those moments of inattentiveness are unrecoverable. The realization that you've been unconscious is itself a moment of consciousness, but for the rest, you might as well have been asleep.

LIFE IS LONG

The walking stupor we call daily life might have significant survival value.

One of the biggest lies you'll ever hear is that "Life is short." If life is short, how can a three-hour movie be interminable? How can a transatlantic flight last for eons? How can a grocery line take forever?

Perceived time may be relative, but life is the longest thing going. Imagine how much longer life would seem if you were conscious all the time.

DREAM/LIFE INTERPRETATION

If we have managed to sufficiently blur the distinction between sleeping, dreaming, and puttering around in a half-conscious daze throughout the day, let us proceed to address the most common dream symbols and see what they have to tell us about our feeble lives.

It is important to note that, with a few exceptions, these dream events mean the same thing whether they happen during sleep or in waking life.

Dream Event/Symbol	Meaning
You've lost your purse.	This has dual meanings. If you're a female, you are feeling at risk of losing control of your life. If you're a male, you should keep your hands closer to your genitals.
Your car has four flat tires.	Your vehicle (i.e., your body) is letting you down. But you're in luck this time and it's nothing that can't be repaired.
You have a school exam that you haven't studied for. In fact, you've forgotten that you enrolled in the class.	Aren't you glad you're not in school anymore?

You are flying through space, enjoying yourself and amazed at your abilities.	This is your dreaming self thumbing its nose at your waking self.
You receive a message from someone who has recently passed away.	Don't listen. Just because they're dead doesn't make them smart.
You encounter a powerful beast—a ram, a stag, or a bear.	Here it matters whether you're dreaming or not. If you're asleep, this is a glimpse of your own potential for strength and power. If you're awake, run like hell.
You are trying to get someplace, but you are unable to move.	That's because you've become temporarily detached from your motor functions. You're either dreaming or you're comatose. If you hear someone calling your name, blink your eyes twice.

Affirmations

• *I am dreaming that I have woken up.*

• *I can't remember why I pinched myself.*

• *I think I'm awake, but it could be a trick.*

13

Cockeyed Optimism

Accentuate the Positive

WHO HAS MORE FUN? The optimist, for whom life never quite meets expectations? Or the pessimist, for whom life is a never-ending series of "I told you so's"?

Trick question, right? There's a trick answer, too.

The secret—which *Wishful Thinking* is now authorized to reveal—is to have no expectations.

It's amazing how responsive the universe is. If you expect the worst, it's easy for life to oblige. And if you expect the best, well, that's asking a lot.

The loophole, again, is *don't expect anything*. If you don't give Them anything to work with, it puts a crimp in their plans for you.

BEYOND HOPE

Does it hurt to hope? Nope.

One might describe the theme of this book as the triumph of hope over experience. Experience, you may have come to realize, is not all it's cracked up to be. It was experience that got us into this mess. Perhaps hope can get us out of it.

In fact, you can go way beyond mere hope. Using techniques such as those described elsewhere in this volume—mocking-up operations, selective and creative memory procedures, blame-fixing, never-minding, glossing-over, and other auto-delusional measures—you need never face an unmet expectation or unfulfilled promise again.

POLLYANNIC PERVERSITY

Is it possible to be *too* positive in your outlook? You bet it is. You don't want to be so confident in your invincibility that you walk out into traffic or invest in technology stocks.

Here are a few ways to recognize when you're being overly Pollyannic in your perspective:

• You're always pointing out the bright side of other people's problems.

- You're able to see the bright side of your own problems.

- You think everything happens for a reason.

- You believe that every day, in every way, things are getting better and better.

- You took the title of this book seriously for even a moment.

Affirmations

+ *I'm as corny as Kansas in August.*

+ *Everything always works out for the best.*

+ *No matter what happens, I'm not going to change.*

14

Follow Your Intuition

Knowing What's Good for You

INTUITION IS MAGIC.

Just say the word, and people who wouldn't dream of consulting a psychic reader, palmist, or clairvoyant will spend thousands on an intuitive counselor, an intuitive business advisor, or an intuitive shopping consultant.

Intuition is huge.

There are hundreds of odd (some very odd) books on awakening, developing, training, enhancing, perfecting, and fine-tuning your intuition. There are books on intuition in business, in medicine, in science, in music, in art, in mathematics, in love, and in your dreams. Other books teach you intuitive leadership, intuitive investing, intuitive healing, intuitive cooking, intuitive psychotherapy, intuitive management, intuitive lovemaking . . . to name just a few.

It is amazing how deeply intuition has penetrated the mainstream and been accepted as a viable approach to decision making. It's like a giant loophole in the laws of common sense and reason that guide modern society.

THE INTUITION JUGGERNAUT

How, you might ask, does intuition differ from traditional methods of psychic awareness such as clairvoyance and precognition?

The answer is that intuition has made an end run around science and parapsychology with claims beyond those ever dared by any paranormal researcher. It's parapsychology without tears.

Normal paranormal talents such as telepathy are notoriously capricious and unreliable. Just when you think you've found a gifted subject, he or she will fail utterly to perform—especially before an audience of skeptics.

Intuition, on the other hand is *never wrong*—as one of its more enthusiastic practitioners put it. If you do get a wrong answer, it wasn't your intuition you were using. Pretty convenient, wouldn't you say?

UNDERLYING ASSUMPTIONS

Whether your intuitions are messages from your subconscious, from your higher self, or from an outside agency, they are always supposed to be *beneficial* in the most unapproachable, untestable, and blindly optimistic sense of the word.

Does this mean beneficial for you, for your family, for your bankbook, for your creditors, for your community, for your company, for society, for the planet? Who knows? Who cares?

Like a chess master who can see all possible moves and always make the best choice, so intuition can cut through the uncertainty and unpredictability of life and illuminate a clear path to your goal, however obscure that goal may be to your conscious mind.

Sounds pretty good, right? So how do you do it?

TOOLS FOR INTUITION: The Pit and the Pendulum

Most writers suggest that, when attempting to consciously manifest intuitive insights, you relax and try to achieve a receptive and open mental and emotional state such as we've described in almost every chapter of this book.

You then proceed to put your inquiry in the form of a question. The exact query is of little importance to the process, but it's usually suggested that it be answerable with a "yes" or a "no": Will I ever marry? Should I eat this carrot? Is this a reliable technique?

In the literature devoted to developing and applying intuition, these procedures and tools are mentioned most frequently:

- *The Pit.* Many people feel that the first indication of an intuitive "hit" can be felt in the pit of your stomach. A queasy feeling can be an indication that you are about to make a bad decision. Alternatively, it can mean that you already made one when you decided to eat that extra slice of pepperoni pizza.

- *The Pendulum.* For those who require the trappings of objective verification, or who believe that the use of instrumentation in some way increases the accuracy of the guesswork, some recommend the use of a pendulum. (Any weight at the end of a string will do.) The pendulum acts as an amplifier of your unconscious tendencies—the inner you that knows the right answer. While appearing to try to hold it steady, you actually swing it in whichever direction you want. One direction means "yes," the other "no."

- *Eye Rolling.* Ask yourself a question while looking in the mirror. If your eyes roll counterclockwise, it means the answer is "no." If your eyes roll clockwise, it means that you are going to proceed against your better judgment.

• *The Pinocchio Effect*. Again, ask yourself a question while looking in the mirror. Answer the question. If your nose grows perceptibly, you're lying to yourself.

When it comes to the power of intuition to affect positive change in your life, we've only just scratched the surface. For more, read my forthcoming book, *Wishful Thinking through Intuition* or *Intuition through Wishful Thinking*. I'll consult my pendulum to decide which title will have better sales.

Affirmations

- *Something tells me I'm on the right track.*

- *I will always trust answers arrived at without sufficient understanding.*

- *What's good for me is good for everyone.*

Internet Research Results

"*Intuition is how your brain uses your other five senses.*"

"*Intuition is part of your birthright, your instructions from a Higher Power, or whatever you choose to call God.*"

"*Intuition is a high-skill area of Corporate Mystics.*"

"*Intuition is a growth, primarily, in sensitivity and in an inner response to the soul.*"

"*Intuition is direct apprehension of truth, or perhaps one should say, the feeling of direct apprehension of truth.*"

"*Intuition is an 'idiot's art.' Intuition does not require that you 'know' anything about the subject that you're reading. It doesn't even require that you understand the impressions you're receiving!*"

"*Intuition is unreliable because the conscious mind can confuse predictive deduction by intuition with other subconscious procedures.*"

"*True divine intuition is difficult to attain on earth in a dense physical body.*"

"*Intuition is our link with other worlds.*"

"*Intuition is found in the spaces between your thoughts.*"

"*Intuition is weird.*"

"*Intuition is a significant instance of prehension, which is central to a process form of pluralistic idealism that some of us consider the crowning achievement of the rational, reflective activity of humanity.*"

"*Intuition is a word that science may fully define one day.*"

"*Intuition is the subconscious response to reason, whereby knowledge beyond reason is attained.*"

"*Intuition is a muscle that can be trained.*"

"*Intuition is the most intuitive thing intuitive intuitives can intuit to have intuition, one must be intuitive . . .*" *(Okay. This one is a gimmick to trick the search engines.)*

"*Intuition is the psychological function that the child uses while in the womb.*"

"*Intuition is what results when we allow our five senses to mingle freely with each other.*"

"*Intuition is tricky business.*"

15

Full Immunity

Mind-Body Hijinks

IF IT WERE UP TO you or me to consciously perform even the most rudimentary bodily functions, we'd be in big trouble. I don't know how to digest food or, God forbid, circulate blood. The electrochemical processes necessary to, say, dissolve a breath mint are way beyond my wildest imaginings.

If you were told that your firstborn would be slain unless you produced some earwax, you'd be thankful indeed that your body knows how to do it—because you certainly don't.

And if you cut your finger or scrape your knee, you don't need help from your doctor, your therapist, or your psychic surgeon. It will take care of itself.

All healing is miraculous.

We can create theories of self-organization, autopoesis, ectoplasmic residue, or biomorphic resonance,[8] but what it comes down to is that, left alone, living organisms tend to heal themselves.

The problem, of course, is that it's nearly impossible to leave them alone. The mind, that hyperactive chatterbox located behind your eyes, insists on having its say. And in so doing, it complicates matters no end.

DO YOU MIND?

How does the mind affect the healing process? Well, firstly, it tries to fix things. Since, as we've pointed out (a) things would most likely fix themselves and (b) we don't have the faintest idea what we're doing, chances are what we do to fix things will only make matters worse. If we do manage to make ourselves better through our own ministrations, it's dumb luck (or serendipity, angelic intervention, intuitive self-support, divine guidance, or scientific mumbojumbo, depending on which chapter we're in).

Another thing the mind will do is delude itself. In fact, of all the mind's functions, the one that works most efficiently is its capacity for self-deception. We are at our best when we're blowing things out of proportion, missing the point, failing to see the big picture, overlooking the obvious, following

8. These are real theories.

false leads, forgetting what we just learned, heeding wrong advice, and arriving at erroneous conclusions.

KNOW THYSELF

One of the mind's widely heralded faculties is its ability to influence the body's immune system. Unlike the circulatory system or the musculature, the immune system is amorphous and theoretical and, as such, is notoriously open to psychological suggestion. (Perhaps the only one of the body's systems to be more prone to disruption from mental messages is the eliminatory system, as anyone knows who has ever competed in a golf tournament.)

The immune system is that which recognizes and distinguishes what is me (or you) from what is not me (or not you). Quite literally, when your self-esteem is low, your boundaries become less well-defined, and your body is less able to discriminate between the various substances and influences that act upon it.

WHAT'S A BODY TO DO?

Warning: Don't read this shortly before or shortly after eating.

On the bright side, your body is not really yours. It's not even really a body. It's actually a teeming swarm of organisms, uni- and multi-cellular creatures, hulking, armored mini-insects, crab-like micro-carnivores, skin- and hair-eating demodex mites, various and sundry bacteria and multifarious microbes and mitochondria. Each of your cells is, in fact, capable of an independent, albeit short and boring, existence.

With the help of your own creative imagination, these creatures conspire to perpetuate the illusion of a cohesive corpus, a separate and identifiable self. (It's a wonder you're even able to read this book.)

For optimum health, you need to get a majority of these entities on your side. The whole system acts as a democracy, with all of the corruption and influence peddling that this implies. Thank goodness it's not a republic, or major parts of you would be bloated while other portions would be woefully underfed.

SOME DO'S AND DON'TS FOR STRENGTHENING YOUR IMMUNE SYSTEM

As immunity is such a hot-button topic these days, we offer a little practical, everyday advice, gleaned from our mountains of research, for optimizing your immune system for health and longevity:

Don'ts	Do's
Don't eat fresh vegetables. They come from the ground, where dead people are buried.	Do eat canned food. Overcooking is your first line of defense against germs.
Don't eat grains. They are small and can get stuck in your throat.	Do eat lamb, followed by milk. It's not kosher, but it lines your body with a protective layer of congealed fat.
Don't drink water. Fish fuck in it. [9]	Do drink alcohol. It is an antiseptic and cleanses your system.
Don't take vitamins. They are unnatural and will bring down the wrath of the nature deities.	Do smoke cigarettes. This will cauterize your lungs and protect you against airborne pestilence.
Don't exercise. It wears out your body and opens your pores to bacteria and other filth.	Do watch plenty of TV. There are so many good shows on now.

Affirmations

* *If I have to choose between my mind and my body, I will.*

* *Out goes the bad, in comes the good.*

* *We, your body's cells, are all happy as clams.*

9. Which is why W.C. Fields never touched the stuff.

16

A Diagnostic Grab Bag

Past Lives, Alien Abduction, Satanic Abuse, et al.

THERAPISTS, LIKE OTHERS in the helping professions, are most effective when dealing in their own areas of specialization. Naturally, their knowledge is constantly augmented with new discoveries, and their specialties often reflect the latest trends in psychological theory.

Modern diagnoses frequently go beyond those identified in the psychological manuals. Depending upon the practitioner, clients nowadays can suffer from multiple personality disorder, spirit attachment and possession, past-life trauma, repressed memories of abuse, alien abduction, perforated aura, chakra imbalance, psychic attack, satanic ritual abuse, astrological affliction, and who knows what other newly discovered maladies?

To aid in these dianoses, hypnosis has become widely used as a therapeutic tool, especially for "recovering" the memories of recalcitrant patients, i.e., those who don't readily concur with their therapist's predispositions. Here are three actual case histories that demonstrate this principle:

Case History 1: Past-Life Trauma

From the notes of Dr. Grace Grace, Ph.D.:

The patient Randall, a 24-year-old male, was referred to me by Dr. S. Simon, who suspected that Randall's symptoms might be the result of past-life trauma (PLT). Randall presented with several symptoms indicative of PLT, including difficulty sleeping, inability to commit to a relationship, feelings of inadequacy, sadness, and acne.

With the patient's consent, I commenced a hypnotic session. According to the usual and accepted procedure, the patient was induced to relax and was soon in a deep trance. The following exchange took place seven minutes into the session:

—What are you thinking?

—*I'm thinking about being here, with you, in this chair.*

—Forget about me. I find it interesting that you're thinking about the chair. Is it comfortable?

—*Very.*

—Is it just physically comfortable, or is it comfortable because it's familiar?

—*I don't know, it's just comfortable.*

—So you don't remember ever being in a chair like this before?

—*I don't know. I don't think so.*

—But it's possible, yes?

—*Yes.*

—If you can't recall it, maybe it's because it happened so long ago that you can't remember. Do you think that's possible?

—*I guess so.*

—If you've never sat in this chair before, don't you find it strange that it would be so familiar?

—*Yes, it is strange, I guess.*

—Maybe you have sat in it, but at a much, much earlier time. I want you to remember yourself sitting in this chair at some other time.

—*Okay.*

—What are you wearing?

—What am I wearing? Oh, I see what you're getting at. Let's see . . . I'm wearing a sort of military coat, and my hand is inside the front. I'm really short . . .

The patient Randall proceeded to recall a past life as Napoleon. In future sessions, it was revealed that he was actually Josephine. With this realization he was empowered to seek a sex-change operation, which decision he has recently begun to regret.

Case History 2: Satanic Ritual Abuse

From the notes of Dr. Clarence Clarence, Ph.D.:

Patient Georgia D., 19, was referred to me by Dr. S. Stuart, who suspected that Georgia was a possible victim of satanic ritual abuse (SRA). Georgia presented with symptoms indicative of SRA, including problems in her home life, insomnia, a sense of failure, mild depression, and acne.

I encouraged the patient to undergo hypnosis, to which she agreed. Accordingly, I hypnotized Georgia with the usual procedures. I then regressed her to childhood. This exchange took place twelve minutes into the session:

—Do you remember ever being in a room with your parents?

—Yes.

—Aha! Is there anyone else in the room with them?

—*No.*

—Are you sure?

—*I don't think so.*

—You don't think anyone else is there, or you don't think you're sure?

—*I don't know.*

—Is it possible that somebody else is there?

—*Maybe.*

—Good. What are they doing, these other people?

—*I don't remember.*

—You don't remember, or you don't want to remember? Are they touching you improperly?

—*I don't think so.*

—But you're not sure.

—*I don't know.*

—Well, then how are they touching you?

—*Um.*

—Perhaps they are wearing masks?

—*I guess.*

—And they are chanting?

—*Uh.*

—What are they chanting?

—*I can't make it out.*

—They're calling up the devil and his disciples, aren't they?

—*Uh, I guess it's possible.*

From there, Georgia progressed rapidly. She was convinced to sever relations with her family and initiate civil proceedings against her parents to recover the cost of her analysis. Unfortunately, criminal charges were never filed as the district attorney remained unconvinced as to the existence of the satanic cult involving Georgia's parents and their friends and associates.

Case History 3: Alien Abduction

From the notes of Dr. Lewis Lewis, Ph.D.:

The patient F., female (34), was referred to me by Dr. C. Clark, who suspected that F.'s case was one of alien abduction (AA). F.'s symptoms were persistent but not severe. All were consistent with known symptoms of AA. They included mild sleep disorder, a failed marriage, loneliness, occasional feelings of inferiority, ennui, and acne.

I told the patient that a hypnotic session is often useful. She agreed to try it, and I proceeded to induce a relaxed state, followed by a deep trance. The diagnosis followed from this revealing exchange:

—Did you ever have any imaginary friends when you were a child?

—*No.*

—I'd be much happier if you said yes.

—*Okay. Maybe I did.*

—Don't say it just for my benefit. What did they look like?

—*I don't remember.*

—Did you ever see the movie *E.T.*?

—*Yes.*

—Well, I don't want you to think about that. Now what did your imaginary friends look like?

—*I'm not sure.*

—What were their eyes like?

—*Uh.*

—Picture them in your mind. Were their eyes big or small?

—*I guess big. Yes, and oddly shaped.*

—Don't say so unless it's true. What were their arms like?

—*Their arms were thin, right?*

—Good, now we're getting somewhere.

The patient F. went on to describe the classic Alien Abduction scenario, just like the movie *Communion,* which she had also seen. F. was introduced into our weekly abduction group. She attends meetings regularly and participates in the group's occasional field trips, which occur when landings seem imminent.

Affirmations

• *If it happened in my past life I should forget about it.*

• *My false memories are more traumatic than your false memories.*

• *I will be ready when they come for me.*

17

Alternative Alternative Medicine

The Joys of Juju

IN RECENT YEARS we've seen a great deal of mainstream interest in alternative medicine. Doctors have begun to appreciate the value of a broader, holistic perspective when it comes to health and well-being. Hospitals and clinics now routinely offer such treatments as meditation, massage, and group therapy. Even HMOs are getting into the act if they think it will save them a few bucks.

We are coming to realize that it's not essential that the theory behind a procedure be perfectly understood in order for that procedure to be effective. In both mainstream and alternative medicine, we routinely employ therapies based on what has been observed to work—with the theory coming after the fact, if at all.

SPIRITUAL SPADEWORK

Few doubt that there's value in some—if not all—of the nontraditional approaches now being used to foster the healing process and to make the practice of medicine more humane.

To further investigate this question, *Wishful Thinking* has probed the far reaches of alternative medicine, mainly looking into what is termed "energy medicine." This includes aromatherapy, bioenergetics, chakra therapy, color therapy, crystal healing, flower remedies, gem therapy, homeopathy, iridology, applied kinesiology, magnetic therapy, music therapy, pendulum therapy, polarity therapy, radionics, reflexology, sound therapy, vibrational therapy, and so on.

We have found so much to wade through that there is a danger of throwing the baby out with the bathwater—or the hog with the hogwash, as the case may be.

While some treatments are based on observed effectiveness, many therapies, it seems, proceed from either (a) loosely interpreted ancient lore or (b) purely abstract models concerning chakras, auras, and energy fields. (See chapter 7, Vibration, Chakras, and You.) We might call these practices "faith-based" therapies.

Are such procedures testable? Certainly. There's no reason why some of these protocols couldn't lend themselves to objective verification through clinical trials, blind judging, control groups, and the other trappings of statistical analysis.

The problem is that no one, neither the alternative practitioner nor the straight scientist, has much interest in performing such testing. Both have a lot to lose, and since people on both sides think that they are the sole Executor of God's Will, it doesn't appear that we'll be seeing blind studies any time soon.

Meanwhile, here's a small sampling of what is out there:

DID YOU KNOW?[10]

- If you are born in late February or early March, you tend to catch colds through your feet.

- The tone of G above middle C can be used to manifest greater abundance in your life.

- The long A vowel sound can affect the assimilation of all nutrients and is tied to heart and childhood diseases.

---

10. *Wishful Thinking* makes no claims or assurances as to the accuracy of these statements. What did you think?

- "Color breathing" on a daily basis can be used to balance and strengthen the chakras.

- The color indigo can be used effectively to treat all conditions of the face, including eyes, ears, nose, mouth, and sinuses. It can also awaken devotion and intuition.

- There is a complete map of your body on the bottoms of your feet.

- Quartz crystals can be used to speed healing of broken bones and to open your aura to gifts of the spirit.

- In homeopathy, the smaller the amount of the active ingredient, the stronger the dosage. The highest doses do not contain any of the active ingredient.

- A pendulum held over a person's body can detect disturbances that could cause future disease.

- Frankincense and lilac fragrances are used to purify our subtle bodies in preparing them as separate vehicles of consciousness.

- Blackberry essence can be used to open up new levels of consciousness.

- To diagnose the pathology of a patient using radionics, it is not necessary for the patient to be present.

- The color orange can be used to open one to energies and beings upon the astral plane.

- Deep blue is good for hemorrhoids.

- Gem elixirs are more powerful if you make them in a crystal bowl. Be sure to "chime" the crystal bowl twelve times for the twelve signs of the zodiac.

- Anointing the head with essence of magnolia while meditating will aid in psychic development, especially for finding lost objects.

- Swelling can indicate a clogged attitude or process in life.

- The color powder blue is good for blisters.

- Jasmine can stimulate mental clarity and can help facilitate the birth process.

- Mahler's *Symphony No. 1 in D Major* will stimulate your spleen chakra.

ALTERNATIVE ALTERNATIVE ALTERNATIVE MEDICINE

For the benefit of our readers, *Wishful Thinking* is including fuller explication of the following little-known but highly effective treatment modalities.

Entomotherapy

The healing power of bugs and insects, once known only to shamans, aardvarks, and house cats, is now available to everyone through the use of Entomo-Essences™. To prepare Entomo-Essences™ for self-administration or for dispensing to your clients, insects should be washed and rinsed, lightly killed, oven-dried, and then ground into a fine powder. Entomo-Essences™ may be mixed with apple juice.

The following are the most commonly used insects, along with the symptoms they are known to alleviate:

Ants—for treatment of confusion and disorganization

Bumblebees—for clumsiness

Dragonflies—for overactive imagination

Earwigs—for hearing disorders

Gnats—for irritability

Ladybugs—for lovesickness

Mosquitoes—for skin lesions

Pill Bugs—for placebo effect

Praying Mantis—for direct contact with divinity

Spiders—for phobias

Walking Stick—for arthritis

Candy Therapy

These remedies have been filched from the long-out-of-print volume, *A Grandparent's Guide to Getting Even.* Read all labels carefully. Be aware of adverse reactions. Remember, a little goes a long way.

Big Hunk—for feelings of male inferiority

Bubble Gum—for disillusionment

Candy Cigarettes—for addictive disorder

Chocolate—for sexual dysfunction

Dots—for skin blemishes

Gumdrops—to nurture your inner child

Jawbreakers—for treatment of aggression

JuJuBes—for casting and breaking spells

Mars Bar—for spaciness

Marshmallows—for sleep disorders

Red Hots—for apathy

Sugar Daddy—for coquettishness

Tootsie Roll—for constipation

Hair of the Dog Therapy

The practice of homeopathy, which was purportedly founded by Samuel Hahnemann in the nineteenth century, has its actual roots deep in popular tradition and common knowledge. The theory that "like cures like" has been known for centuries by bartenders, party goers, and carousers the world over.

Airedale—for difficulty breathing

Bloodhound—for circulatory problems

Bulldog—for stubbornness

Chihuahua—for hair loss

Chow—for eating disorders

Cocker Spaniel or Mastiff—for impotence

Dachshund—for intestinal problems

German Shepherd—for passive-aggressive disorder

Hound—for horniness

Pointer—for spiritual guidance

Poodle—for bad hair days

Retriever—for feelings of loss

Schnauzer—for nasal congestion

Setter—for lethargy

Sheepdog—for hirsuteness

Whippet—for sadomasochism

Affirmations

- *If I knock over my crystal and it breaks, it doesn't mean I'm going to die.*

- *I will use a Ouija board to decide what color to wear today.*

- *I won't listen to any music that hasn't been preapproved by my HMO.*

18

Shaman You

Exploring Your Primal Roots

DID I TELL YOU about my book-signing tour in Quito, Ecuador? It was there that I was drugged and kidnapped by the last remaining Maoist group on the face of the planet. When my publisher failed to pay the ransom, I was wrapped in swaddling clothes and set adrift on the Amazon river, where I was found three days later by a shaman from the Meshugge tribe. For the next thirty years I lived and studied with these Indians in their village in the Peruvian Andes. There I learned the secret shamanic techniques that we're going to discuss here...

Thus begin countless tales by contemporary Western writers, most of whom launched their research as scholarly exercises (or in search of psychoactive substances), and proceeded to become enchanted by, immersed in, and eventually initiated into the ritual lives of precivilized indigenous peoples the world over. [11]

The attraction of shamanism for middle-aged Westerners is obvious. There are the drugs. There's the heart-thumping music. There's staying up all night. There's dancing by yourself. All those things you thought you'd never experience again.

MANY HATS

The name *shaman,* which is now used universally, comes originally from the Tungus people of Siberia. They are closely related to the early Icelanders who gave us the word "ugg," from which all language is derived.

The shaman performs many important functions in tribal life—especially tribal nightlife. Since most villages lack television, nightclubs, live theater, emergency rooms, a red-light district, crack houses, shooting galleries, and sanctioned WWF wrestling events, the shaman has to be all things to all people:

- *Chief medical officer.* As medicine man or witch doctor, the shaman must keep up with the herbal pharmacopoeia, supervising the gathering,

11. A quick check of Amazon—the website, not the river—shows more than 200 recent books with "Shaman" in the title.

storage, and dispensing of medicinal plants, seeds, and roots. Unfortunately, this often leads him to an exaggerated sense of his own importance and a tendency to confuse himself with God.

- *Drug kingpin.* Getting high is as universal a drive as any human instinct. Years of experimentation and talking with the plant spirits have led shamans to some highly refined knowledge about psychoactive substances and their effects. Just like in the city, it is by no means unusual for those who supply the drugs to become community leaders.

- *High priest.* Due primarily to his exalted importance as dispenser of drugs, the shaman is seen by the stoners around him as something of a superior being, one with a special connection to both the spirit world and the underworld. The shaman usually does little to disabuse anyone of this notion.

- *Master of ceremonies.* A successful shaman can work the room with the best of them and is always the life of the party. He frequently doubles as deejay and stand-up entertainer.

- *Zookeeper/madame.* Among the shaman's jobs is to set you up with the totemic animal of your dreams. The importance of this relationship cannot be overstated, for what could be more intimate than a bestial, one-on-one liaison in the privacy of your imagination.

ANIMAL POWERS

It is a widely held shamanic belief that humans and animals can transform into one another, and that we are protected by animal spirits in much the same way as we might be protected by guardian angels (chapter 19) or higher-self spirit guides (chapter 6).

Each animal has its own unique qualities, and the shaman helps select your totem animal after reflecting on your character and your needs. These spirit animals are apt to visit you often, even after you return to daily life, so be careful who you take on as a companion.

- *Coyotes,* for instance, are known as tricksters. You wouldn't want to leave them alone with your stuff.

- *Bears* are fine as long as you stay on their good side. They come in handy in a bar brawl.

- *Snakes* are often considered messengers from on high, so having one as your totem animal is like having a direct spiritual connection. They are also considered symbols of death and rebirth, so keep on the lookout for signs that you might have died.

- *Eagles* are considered intermediaries between heaven and earth. They are also said to be keepers of esoteric wisdom, so if you like to be the one in your circle who doles out the secrets, the eagle is your man.

- *Wolves* are rapacious predators. If you're single, you might find this useful, but if you're married, it could get you in trouble.

- *Swine* are trayf. Sure, sows are considered symbols of fertility and boars have nice tusks, but I'd see if I could trade in for something with more cachet.

- *Deer* are swift and elusive, but they're a little gentle to be protectors of much of anything. Stags, of course, are a different story, what with all that musk and those antlers.

Other animals—crows, turtles, horses, bats, owls, goats, to name a few— have their own quirks and peculiarities. For an unbiased assessment of the essential nature of the beast you're considering, ask any kid.

THE SHAMANIC TRANCE

The spirit journey is at the heart of the shamanic experience. The images and encounters of this trance state, unlike most drug-induced reveries, are predictable and can be manipulated by your accomplished shamanic guide. If you believe the hype, the content of your journey—what visions you see and which animals drop in to chat—is a direct result of the ingredients in your psychedelic stew, and can be further fine-tuned with well-timed utterances and psychic intercession on the part of the shaman.

Nor is it necessarily through drugs that trance is induced. The shaman is an expert at monotony and cacophony. Hours of inexpert drumming, rattling, and dancing are enough to send even the most trance-resistant subject into a near comatose state. The jungle *caca-phone,* a native instrument that sounds as bad as it sounds, is used when the drums don't do the job.

SHAMANIC HEALING

A good portion of our prescription medicine is derived from the plants of the rain forest. While modern practice is to isolate and extract the active ingredients from these plants in the hope of synthesizing them in the laboratory, the shaman uses the entire plant, usually in careful combination with other ingredients. The healing potential of these concoctions is known to the shaman not through experiment but through teachings from the animal spirits, the ancients, the ETs—in fact, whoever shows up during the trance to reveal their secrets.

Modern students of shamanic practice often express hope that such traditional healing techniques will be accepted to the point where they become integrated into Western medicine. We agree. What could be more healing than to see your doctor dolled up with face paint and dancing around your hospital bed?

SUBURBAN SHAMANISM

Chances are you won't be going to the Amazon basin or the Siberian tundra any time soon. So we're going to show you how to throw your own shamanic slumber party without leaving the comfort of your middle-class suburban home.

Here's what you'll need:

Drums	Pots and pans, garbage pails, a corrugated box; almost anything you can bang on will do. Use metal and wooden spoons as drumsticks.
Rattles	A half-filled jar of lentils or pinto beans makes a great rattle. One of those bamboo "rain sticks" would add to the effect.
Face Paint	Lipstick or that stuff football players use will work fine.
Sound Effects	You should be able to get good jungle sound effects at any New Age bookshop. If not, check Amazon—the website *or* the river.

Ayahuasca or Peyote	This might be a little difficult. Here's a recipe for a substitute mixture that should have the same effect:

1 package chocolate pudding
12 mushrooms, sliced
2 ounces tomato paste
6 ounces Drano
6 ounces battery acid
4 tablespoons mystery ingredient*
*email *wishfulthinking@hypersphere.com* for details

Cave	A dark closet will do. You might want to stuff a towel under the door to block out any ambient light.
Fire	Use the fireplace, barbecue, or an approved camp fire area. *Don't light a fire in the closet.*
Stuffed Animals	A good cross section.

Your slumber party should be spontaneous, so we're not going to provide too much in the way of instructions. If you can do it outdoors, on a full-moon night, so much the better. You can draw straws to see who gets to be shaman, or just pick the person with the largest head.

Of course, we don't recommend that you use any illegal substances, but you'll have a much better time if you do.

Affirmations

* *The more uneducated the source, the deeper the knowledge.*

* *The more zoned out I am, the closer I am to God.*

* *I knew there would be drugs in here somewhere.*

19

Guardian By My Side

Or, How Many Angels Can Dance on the Head of a Moron?

EVERY CULTURE old enough to have a tradition has a belief in angelic visitation and intervention. Every religion worth its salt describes a hierarchy of celestial beings. Thousands upon thousands of people have described personal contact with angels or other ethereal messengers whose purpose is to guide, protect, and console us in times of need. Some of the finest artists, writers, and visionaries in history have chosen angels, archangels, and other ministering spirits as the subject of their creations. Nearly five thousand books in print and more than two million websites deal with the subject of angels in one way or another. A Gallup poll on the subject showed that while only 30 percent of Americans questioned believe in ghosts, 25 percent in astrology, and 12 percent in channeling, 72 percent believe in the existence of angels.

Yet in popular culture, in our schools, and in the news media, the very idea of angels, or any form of spirit intervention, is inevitably something of a joke. [12]

GUARDIAN VARIETY ANGELS

Angelologists (whose subject is elusive at best) insist that we draw a distinction between angels—who are messengers of the divine—and other fabulous but inferior creatures such as ghosts, pixies, fairies, wraiths, and so on that pervade our literature and lore. We'll have to take their word for it.

They also draw clear and remarkably well-informed distinctions among the angels themselves.

Guardian angels, the kind we're most likely to encounter at the bank or in the grocery line, are said to be the lowliest of the breed, but they are still representatives of heaven and so have a certain amount of clout. Their job is to protect our sorry asses, to guide us, and to intervene in our lives in beneficial ways.

Other types of angels—powers, dominions, thrones, cherubim, etc.—have their own duties and responsibilities. Some fight demons. Some dispense miracles. Some dispense justice. Some administer the angelic-duty roster. Some are keepers of the celestial records. Some clean up after the horses that

---

12. If any of you reading this happen to *be* angels, we mean no offense.

There are certain ways to tell if your guardian angel is around:

1 You make a costly mistake at work, but it gets blamed on someone else and you get off scot-free.
2 The girl with crabs decides to go home with your friend instead of you.
3 You are about to rob a convenience store when a nun shows up.
4 You slice a five iron terribly, but somehow the ball ends up six inches from the hole.
5 You're about to jump off a bridge when someone comes up to you and reveals how much worse the world would be without you in it.

---

pull the heavenly chariots. The highest of them all, the seraphim, do nothing but surround the throne of God, ceaselessly singing "Holy, Holy, Holy."

THE MODERN VIEW

The contemporary take on angels is deeply confused. On the one hand, angels are a widely accepted and warmly embraced harkening to a purer, more innocent time. But in modern literature or film, angels are almost always treated as fantasy or humor. In academic, intellectual, and scientific circles—in fact, in the eyes of anyone who requires concrete evidence before believing in something—the whole world of discarnate entities, in general, and angels, in particular, is unworthy of serious consideration.

So belief in angels is something of a dirty little secret that most people share but don't talk about (except to Gallup pollsters). The question is, are the millions, perhaps billions, who believe in angels onto something? Or is this just the same sort of mass psychosis that leads to the popularity of Britney Spears?[13]

As Anatole France wrote, "If a million people believe a foolish thing, it is still a foolish thing."

YOUR CREDULITY QUOTIENT

Face it. If you believe wholeheartedly in angels, you've already come a long way toward achieving what this book is about. There's not much more we can teach you about wishful thinking, and you're probably already giving seminars on the subject and making more money than we are.

Wishful Thinking's own informal poll on the question of angels revealed surprising results. Mainly, we never realized how indecisive and wishy-washy our friends are.

While very few were able to say "I believe in angels," neither did anyone volunteer to write off the idea that angels might exist. Though none whom we spoke with had ever experienced any sort of explicit angelic encounter,

---

13. Note to Editor: If this person is no longer popular, replace with current vapid, ridiculous, and extraordinarily popular figure.

most were holding out for the possibility that one or more miraculous or propitious events in their lives might have been the result of divine intervention.

So this "angels" question turns out to be useful as a sort of litmus test. While perhaps made easier by the fact that people throughout history have shared a belief in angels, it remains a confirmation of one's faith—not something contradicted by the evidence, but something believed in the absence of any real evidence beyond personal reports.

DRAWING THE LINE

Do *you* believe in angels? What about ghosts? How about the tooth fairy?

Back in high school, we had this fastidious teacher known for his grumpiness and short temper. Two minutes after class began, a noticeably scruffy student walked into the room and took a seat. The teacher "harrumphed" but said nothing. A few minutes later, a mangy dog wandered into the classroom. "Would somebody please remove that dog?" said the teacher. "We have to draw the line somewhere."

Let us take advantage of the angel debate, expanding it to define and identify our wider beliefs regarding the invisible world.

For each of the entities in the following list, indicate your level of belief according to the following scale:

1. No way.

2. I doubt they exist, but I'm holding back in case I'm wrong.

3. I couldn't say for sure, but I could be bribed to go either way.

4. I'm pretty sure they exist. I've seen pictures.

5. I'm certain they exist. I've had dinner with them.

__ Angels	__ Gnomes	__ Ogres
__ Archangels	__ Goblins	__ Pixies
__ Cherubim	__ Gremlins	__ Quarks
__ Demons	__ Gryphons	__ Satyrs
__ Devils	__ Harpies	__ Sprites
__ Dragons	__ Imps	__ Succubi
__ Dryads	__ Incubi	__ Trolls
__ Elves	__ Leprechauns	__ Unicorns
__ Fairies	__ Mermaids	__ Vampires
__ Ghouls	__ Nymphs	__ Werewolves[14]

Those of you with more convoluted belief systems might find this exercise too simplistic. For instance, perhaps you believe in wood nymphs, but you draw the line at water nymphs. Or perhaps you are too sophisticated or too cool to believe in anything. Or perhaps your belief system permits you to allow for the possibility of anything but the actuality of nothing.

One thing is certain. If you don't believe in the possibility of a thing, you wouldn't recognize it if it smacked you in the face.

Affirmations

- *If it weren't for my imaginary friend here, I would have gone crazy.*

- *If I jump off a building, my guardian angel will catch me.*

- *My guardian angel told me to do it.*

14. Scoring your Drawing the Line exercise:

    0–10 You are probably a very boring person.

  11–40 You really are rather noncommittal, aren't you?

  41–80 You took your scary childhood reading far too seriously.

  81–120 You look over your shoulder a lot, don't you?

121–150 Please check yourself into a nearby Newage Treatment Facility.

20

Changing Channels

Hello, Who's That Speaking Please?

HAVE YOU EVER been to a séance or been in a room with someone who's channeling? If you're like me—and I can only assume you are—it can be quite a test of your self-control.

The first premise of channeling, which is otherwise known as spirit medium-ship or clairaudience, is that someone other than the person sitting in the room with you—someone who has no body of their own—is actually speaking, using the body and voice of the medium or channel.

The second premise of channeling, if you can get past the first, is that the disembodied speaker is a higher being, one with near omniscience when it comes to answering both earthly and spiritual questions.

There are few, if any, tests you can perform to verify the authenticity of the spirit guide.[15] Ultimately, the only criterion for judging the truth and value of a channeled communication is the content of the session.

Channeling is not for the faint of heart, but it's ideal for the faint of mind. While some say that anyone can be a channel, others insist that it takes many years—or even many lifetimes—to prepare yourself to vacate the premises so completely as to be an effective channel.

THE WT SESSION

For the remainder of this chapter, *Wishful Thinking* invited a group of higher beings to contribute via a gifted spirit medium, Madame Sylvia, who offers her telephone-based services via late-night cable television and the Internet. Here is a transcript of that communication:[16]

—*We who are writing this chapter greet you. You humans, especially those of you who come from the shallow end of the gene pool, have much to learn from us.*

WT: Thank you for helping with our book.

---

15. You could try the "eye rolling" test described in chapter 14, Follow Your Intuition.

16. This session is rather short because the telephone charges were very high. We had to pay for twenty-five minutes on hold while Madame Sylvia was summoning up her spirit guides.

— De nada.

WT: I'm a little unsure what questions to ask. We would like to learn more about channeling. Where would you suggest we begin?

— It does not matter where you begin. Nothing you say is of any importance. We have spent many incarnations preparing this material. Do not interrupt.

WT: Who are you?

— We are [unintelligible], of the fifth level. Perhaps you have heard of us.

WT: How do we know you're not just Madame Sylvia herself, or some lower-level spirit functionary?

— That's for us to know and you to find out.

WT: Are you willing to answer our questions?

— We know all of your questions and all of the answers, but we are only going to reveal that which is best for your development. Do you believe that? We'll tell you another one.

WT: How are you able to contact this channel?

— We get many channels here. We have satellite. Ha ha.

WT: Since you are able to speak through Madame Sylvia, can you control her hand gestures and other body movements as well?

—*We can control this medium's body as we so choose, but we are old and have no interest in any of your lowly bodily functions. It would be nice to be able to pee regularly, however.*

WT: Don't you have bodies of your own?

—*We used to have bodies. We misplaced them. Did I say we are old?*

WT: Are you Madame Sylvia's higher self?

—*No. Many so-called channels are doing nothing more than contacting their higher selves or their guardians such as you describe in your pitiful chapter 6. This doesn't count. True channeling has to be contact with those of us here on the fifth level, or higher.*

WT: You keep referring to the fifth level. The fifth level of what?

—*Do not importune. We will tell you what you need to know.*

WT: Can you tell us something we don't already know?

—*Your publisher is planning to remainder your book. Hah. How could we know that if we were not truly great?*

WT: I thought humility is one of the qualities of you higher beings.

—*Shut up. What do you know of higher beings?*

WT: Would it be all right if I were to ask you a personal question?

—*Yes, as long as it's a question about you and not about us. We don't like to talk about ourselves. Much.*

WT: Well, can you tell me something about myself that you think will help me?

—*We see that you are more sensitive than people realize. And that you sometimes worry about money. There is someone important to you whose name begins with a J or a D. You would like to take a vacation. How are we doing?*

WT: That's remarkable. How can you know these things?

—*We can see the past, present, and future unfolding like a paper fan. You are in one of the creases.*

WT: If our readers are interested in asking you their own personal questions, how can they contact you?

—*We thought you would never ask. Just have your readers call our 900 telephone number.[17] We will be happy to answer all of their questions. Your credit card limit has been reached. Please enter another card number to continue this session.*

---

17. Mention *Wishful Thinking* for a 10-percent discount on your first call.

Affirmations

- *If someone's voice sounds funny, they might be channeling.*

- *If you have a frog in your throat, ask it to grant you three wishes.*

- *I will trust the word of anybody who says they don't have a body.*

- *I didn't mean to say that. I was channeling.*

21

The Healing Power of Confusion

The Scientific Basis for Wishful Thinking

MODERN PHYSICS has been a godsend for the self-help business. Since science is the ultimate arbiter of what's real these days, it has been reassuring indeed to find our most cherished assumptions and beliefs supported by the findings—if not the practitioners—of science.

At the basis of these beliefs is the idea that *anything can happen;* no matter how bad things get, they can always change in miraculous ways.

Scientific support for this notion comes from the realization that nobody can predict anything with absolute certainty—a phenomenon known as *quantum indeterminacy.* Unfortunately, physicists, with their narrow worldview, have limited the application of this discovery to such boring areas as measuring the position or velocity of electrons. They maintain that indeterminacy applies only at the quantum level, inside of the atoms and molecules that make up the world.

But the world doesn't *belong* to science. This is your world. These are your atoms, your molecules, your quanta. Who's to say that this same indeterminacy principle can't apply to your golf score, the course of your illness, or your chance of winning the lottery?

The key is to *make quantum unpredictability work for you.*

"These quanta are so small," you should say to yourself, "I can make them do anything I want."

And you don't even have to know what you're doing. As we pointed out in chapter 15, you don't have to understand the process of digestion in order to eat, do you? In fact, there are some things we'd rather not know.

You needn't even have any idea what I'm talking about to take advantage of quantum indeterminacy. Perhaps you're one of those people whose eyes glaze over at the mere mention of anything scientific. No matter. In fact, this probably helps.

Just remember this: *According to science, anything can happen.* You just have to make sure that what actually does happen is what you want to happen. Piece of cake.

THE RELATIVITY BONANZA

Another area of physics that is a boon to self-helpers is Einstein's famous theory of relativity. While some find it depressing to think that nothing is absolute, there are a number of ways that you can turn relativity to your advantage.

If an authority figure tells you something you don't want to hear, just say to yourself, "What does he know? Everything is relative." (It might be a "she," but they're mostly men, aren't they?)

If you're feeling bad, think to yourself, "Surely there's somebody feeling worse. Everything is relative."

If you can't face some unpleasant truth, think: "What is truth anyway in a world of random forces? Everything is relative."

If you're feeling fat, ugly, poor, boring, tiresome, confused, perplexed, befuddled, naive, shallow, banal, ordinary, dull, facile, stupid, obtuse, ignorant, specious, phony, unemployed, lazy, good for nothing, or any combination of the above, just remember: *Everything is relative.*

TIME'S ARROW

According to those who concern themselves with these things, the equations of physics do not specify a direction for *time.* That is, the equations work equally well with time moving forward or backward.

From here—in a leap of faith worthy of any in this volume—many physicists claim that time is *bidirectional,* and that our view of time as going in only one direction is illusional. At best, our experience of forward-moving time is what is known as a *special case,* that which undergoes, to use philosopher Alfred North Whitehead's phrase, "the formality of actually occurring."

Physicists are scientists, after all, so they must know what they're talking about. Let us share in this faith for a moment to see what it gets us.

The most obvious benefit of bidirectional time would be the chance to go back and correct our mistakes. All right, so nobody's been able to do this as far as we know, but isn't it nice to know that some of the smartest people in the world are working on it?

We might also be able to go forward in time to preview the consequences of our actions, then go back and try to minimize the damage.

All of this is theoretical, of course. But then, so was the atom bomb.

Affirmations

+ *Anything is possible when I don't know what I'm talking about.*

+ *I will ignore the obvious. I will believe the impossible.*

+ *This stuff makes sense when I don't think about it.*

22

Beyond Science

The Way of Hubris

WHILE SCIENCE can be turned to our advantage through a liberal interpretation of its findings (as we did in chapter 21), it is often granted greater sovereignty than it deserves. The credulous, unexamined faith that people have in the authority of science is itself a form of wishful thinking.

Not that science is wrong. It's just beside the point. The most important things in life—the beauty of a sunset, the meaning of a poem, the joy of a ball game—are so far outside the realm of science and reason as to be of a different world entirely.

Where science does err is in forgetting its limited purview. Despite what we might hear on television, *nature is not science*. The plants and animals, the weather, the planets, and the stars would all do very well—better in fact—without our interference.

Nor is it always appropriate to use science as a yardstick for what is real. How can we say that an idea such as reincarnation is not valid because it can't be explained by science? Science can't even explain how we can be born *once*.

"We're really only just molecules," said Carl Sagan, a leading promulgator of the view that science has all the answers. He might as well have said, "A Shakespeare play is really only just words." It is this kind of reductionist thinking that raises Missing the Point to the status of religion.

So while science may not often be wrong, scientists frequently are.[18]

---

18. It's not only scientists who are prone to reductionism. This is one of my favorite stories:

A young student approached his spiritual teacher and asked, "What does the universe rest on?"
"That is a good question, my child," replied the teacher. "It rests on the back of a large elephant."
"But what is the elephant standing on?" asked the student.
"It is standing on the backs of four turtles," said the teacher.
"And what are the turtles standing on?" asked the student.
"They are standing on four rocks," said the teacher, now clearly annoyed.
"But what are the rocks standing on?" the student insisted.
"Young man," said the teacher, "it's rocks all the way down."

EDIFICE COMPLEX

More often it is the otherwise intelligent layperson (such as yourself) who makes the mistake of imagining that science has the ultimate answers. In this view, it is only a matter of time before science has filled in the blanks in our understanding of the world. When the edifice of knowledge is complete, we will be able to predict with certainty anything to which we put our brilliant little minds.

But it was science itself that revealed the insubstantiality of the material world. The edifice that we are hoping to construct is, like the atom, mostly empty space—or in this case, hot air.

There are deep limitations, both theoretical and practical, in our ability to know and predict the behavior of the physical world, not to mention the living world. The idea that "any day now" we will have a Theory of Everything, or of *anything* significant for that matter, is no more or less grounded than the idea that fairies are about to swoop down and take all your troubles away.[19]

---

19. You might think I'm making this up, but a Google search for "Theory of Everything" revealed 18,600 hits.

THE SCIENTIST SPECULATES

But lest we overbuild our straw man, we should point out that not all scientists share in this absolute, if misplaced, faith in the system.

This story is told about Niels Bohr, the Danish physicist and founder of quantum theory:

A visiting journalist notices that the famous scientist has a horseshoe over his doorway.

"Surely, Professor Bohr," says the writer, "a scientist such as you doesn't believe that a horseshoe will bring good luck."

"No, of course not," replies Bohr. "But I understand it works even if you don't believe in it." [20]

The greater the scientist, the deeper the thinker, the more likely he or she will deviate from the stereotype and surprise us with open-mindedness and breadth of interest.

So, if we may drop the irony and wax unfunny for a moment, allow us to offer these . . .

20. According to some, it was Bohr himself who told this story about a neighbor. Niels Bohr's model of the atom was featured, in simplified form, in the 1950s Disney film *Our Friend the Atom*.

Affirmations for Scientists

- *I will leave room for the mysteries—of life, of nature, of human relations, of mind, of spirit—and I will leave open the possibility that what I think I know might very well be wrong.*

- *When I hear something new, I will not treat it as something already known, and I will admit, when faced with the evidence, that an idea that I had previously opposed might very well be the case.*

- *I will speculate outside my area of expertise, and I will push my own field into uncharted territory and greater depths.*

- *I will encourage the work of others, even when that work might present a challenge to my own accomplishments and authority.*

- *I will accept the likelihood that we humans are probably far from being the pinnacle of universal creation.*

23

Humor and Prayer

When All Else Fails

"LIFE IS METAPHOR."

Nothing you can say could be more irritating to the true believer.

The idea that interpretation is everything, or that there is no absolute truth, is infuriating to protectors of the faith. It would be like an avid baseball fan saying that Babe Ruth hit 60 home runs in 1927, and you replying, "Yes, probably."

The greatest sin, to these yahoos, is spiritual relativism. The idea of an "as if" world is not acceptable. You're either with us or you're against us (like U.S. foreign policy).[21]

21. In *The Philosophy of "As If"* Hans Vaihinger argued that since reality cannot be truly known, human beings construct systems of thought to satisfy their needs and then assume that actuality agrees with their constructions; i.e., people act "as if" the real were what they assume it to be.

LET US PRAY

For some such persons, and for many others besides, prayer is what you do with the kids by the side of the bed or before dinner. It's what you do in church, at temple, or in your mosque. There's little question as to Whom you are addressing, and your relationship to the divinity is as supplicant to a superior being.

Others, the exemplars for this book, would say that *all* thought is prayer, that the negative and positive mutterings of your mind are projected out into the world and that they shape the world to that image. Explanations for this can either include God or not, depending on the individual.

Still others might say that prayer is meaningless and ineffectual, that only physical action can affect the world. Questions concerning God or metaphysics make such persons edgy and irritable.

Where is the truth? Somewhere in the middle? Or nowhere?

While some people pray to God, some to their personal protective spirit, and some to themselves, prayer helps all these people recognize what they really want, which is no small thing. It's wishful thinking to expect your prayers to be answered, but if you *don't* expect them to be answered, then you haven't got a prayer.

STRANGE BEDFELLOWS

Prayers can heal, or so we've been led to believe. And so can humor, as numerous studies have shown. As little as we understand the healing process, we understand the mechanisms of prayer and humor even less.

What else do humor and prayer have in common?

1. Both draw on a mysterious, little-understood force (though not necessarily the same one).

2. Both provide comfort in times of difficulty.

3. Both get boring when repeated too often.

4. Both are forms of pleading.

5. Both couldn't hurt.

Is this stretching things? Perhaps. What are you going to do about it? The book is almost finished. If it has done its job, and if this "healing power of humor" business is all it's cracked up to be, you should be all better now.

Still have some aches and pains? How about a few prayers?

CAN'T TELL THE PRAYERS WITHOUT A SCORECARD

- God, grant me the wit to deride the things I cannot understand, the savvy to convince others I know what I'm talking about, and the wisdom to know when to shut up.

- Lord give me a sign
  that you can hear me,
  And I'll give you a discount
  on your next haircut.

- Forgive us our trespasses, our peccadilloes, and our dalliances, for these are white collar crimes. Lead us not into temptation unless you're prepared to deliver.

- O Lord,
  what does it take
  to get waited on around here?

- Protect me, dear Lord.
  My feet are so small,
  And your shoes are so big.

- O Lord, convert the world
  —and begin with my partner.

- I seek thy staff to comfort me,
  but I can't figure out thy voicemail system.

- Now I lay me down in bed, I hear these voices in my head. I hope I die
  before my wake, or someone's made a big mistake.

- Forgive me, Lord,
  if I seem distracted.
  You have left me with a lot
  to deal with here.

- Please let me see in advance,
  the course of thy ways
  that I might place a bet on the outcome.

- Praised be thou, O Lord,
  Who hath created email.

- Guide us toward the path of righteousness.
  Or failing that, where can I get a donut?

- Blessed art thou, O Lord our God, King of the Universe,
  for leaving us to figure everything out for ourselves.

Affirmations

- *It doesn't matter to whom I pray as long as I send money.*

- *When I pray, I usually know the answer.*

- *If God doesn't have a sense of humor, I'm in big trouble.*

Recommended Reading

Balderdash, Hokum, and Twaddle
by H. T. Murgetroyd

The Cellophane Prophecy
by Red Jamesfield

Chicken Soup for the Kitchen Table
by Jack Canthit

Dangerous Occult Secrets for the Millions
by Aleister Crumbly

The Grace at the End of the Schlep
by Sheik Katchmi Ifyu Khan

How to Get Up and Get Out of Bed
by Bertha Vanation

The I-Spot: Finding Your Intuition Chakra
by A. W. Malarkey

Inanity for Dummies
by R. U. Kidden

The Intuition Bonanza: Ten Ways You Can Cash In
by Karma Goldfarb

The Self-Reference Book
by I. T. Self

Spiritual Intimidation
by Baba Gin Rumi

Stop Trying: A How-Not-To Book
by Swami Bananananda

The Way of the Yeti: Health and Beauty Tips from the Himalayas
by Lama Llama

A Wisenheimer's Guide to Science
by Y.I. Oughtta

ARTHUR BLOCH is the author of the *Murphy's Law* books, which have been published in more than 30 countries and have sold millions of copies worldwide. Since 1986 he has been producer/director of the *Thinking Allowed* public television series, featuring interviews with many of the world's leading scholars and researchers in areas of personal and spiritual development, philosophy, psychology, and the

PHOTO BY KEITH WALL

frontiers of science. Bloch is the founder of the Wishful Thinking Institute, the Wishful Thinking Spiritual Center, the Wishful Thinking Health and Beauty Spa, the Wishful Thinking Intuitive Consultants Group, the Wishful Thinking Alternative Medicine Clinic, and the Wishful Thinking Dating Service. Bloch also runs Hypersphere, an internet design company. He lives in Oakland, California, with his wife, Barbara.

Visit the *Wishful Thinking* website at www.hypersphere.com/wishfulthinking